2018
FIFA WORLD CUP
RUSSIA™

FACT FILE

Get ready for kick-off

Players, coaches and fans are ready for the greatest football festival on the planet – the 2018 FIFA World Cup™! After hundreds of qualifying games around the globe, 32 teams will battle for the FIFA World Cup Trophy as the biggest superstars in the game chase the ultimate prize. In June and July, host nation Russia will stage the greatest sporting party. Your *2018 FIFA World Cup Russia™ Fact File* has everything you need to know!

Contents

Note to readers: the facts and statistics in this book are accurate as of 1 November 2017.

Welcome to the 2018 FIFA World Cup™

"A dream has come true." That is what Germany goalkeeper Manuel Neuer said after he lifted the FIFA World Cup Trophy in Brazil in 2014. Germany, now captained by Neuer, will again be one of the favourites for success in Russia. Brazil, Spain and Argentina will also fancy their chances of glory, along with dark horses such as the talented Belgium team and a Harry Kane-inspired England.

This is the first FIFA World Cup to be held in Russia. It seems like the perfect setting – the biggest country in the world staging the greatest football event. Across 11 beautiful Russian cities and 12 impressive stadiums, 64 matches will take place between 14 June and 15 July. Football fans are guaranteed at least 5,760 minutes of action, with 11 games during the first four days alone. Legends such as Lionel Messi, Cristiano Ronaldo, Neymar, Thomas Müller and Robert Lewandowski will all be on show, so make sure you do not miss a minute!

Manuel Neuer lifts the FIFA World Cup Trophy in 2014.

Brazil's Neymar, Germany's Thomas Müller and Lionel Messi of Argentina all have their eyes on glory at Russia 2018.

Then and now

The first FIFA World Cup Finals took place in 1930. Hosts Uruguay beat Argentina in the Final and FIFA, the governing body of the game, knew the tournament was a huge success and had vast potential to become popular around the globe. Russia 2018 will be the 21st Finals and in the last 88 years Brazil, Germany, Italy, Argentina, Spain, France and England have all triumphed.

At the 2014 FIFA World Cup in Brazil, a record-equaling 171 goals were scored.

Trophy talk

So why is the FIFA World Cup™ Trophy so special? For a player to get his hands on this legendary prize, he needs to have excelled in the most pressurized games imaginable. He and his team-mates have had to qualify for the Finals, then navigate group and knockout games before being victorious in the Final. The FIFA World Cup™ Trophy was first presented in 1974. It is the most iconic trophy in the world and is 36.8cm tall, weighs 6.142kg and its body and base plate are made from 18-carat gold. Germany have won the FIFA World Cup™ Trophy three times since the 1970s.

Famous players to have lifted the FIFA World Cup™ Trophy include Brazil heroes Pelé and Romário, Argentina's Diego Maradona, Italy's Gianluigi Buffon, Spain superstars Andrés Iniesta and Xavi, France ace Thierry Henry and England captain Bobby Moore. For greats such as Messi, Ronaldo and Neymar, who have yet to taste such glory, could 2018 be the year their dream finally comes true?

The Jules Rimet Cup™ (*right*) was presented at the first FIFA World Cup Finals in 1930. It was in use until 1970, when it was given to Brazil after their third Finals victory.

How the FIFA World Cup™ Finals Work

On 14 June, all eyes will be on the Luzhniki Stadium in Moscow as the 2018 FIFA World Cup Finals begin with Russia playing Saudi Arabia. The host nation always qualifies automatically for the Finals but the other 31 countries had to progress from their regional qualifying groups. Sweden even had a tense two-leg play-off to negotiate. Some great footballing nations, such as Italy and the Netherlands, failed to reach the Finals, which shows just how fierce the qualifying fight was.

The Group Stage

On 1 December 2017, in the historic Kremlin building in Moscow, the draw was made to decide which of the 32 teams would go into each group. There are eight groups, lettered A to H, each with four teams. Each team plays three games in their group, which means football fans get to enjoy a huge 48 group matches. The top two teams in each group progress to the round of 16.

Spain were crowned champions at South Africa 2010 despite losing their first group game.

The Knockout Stage

Pages 62-63 show you how the round of 16 matches are set up, but as an example the country that finishes top in Group A will play the team that comes second in Group B. From here on, all games are knockout matches. This means that only the winning team progresses. If the score is tied after 90 minutes, there will be 30 minutes of extra time. If the game is still level after extra time, a penalty shoot-out decides the winner. There will then be four quarter-finals, two semi-finals, a third-place play-off and finally the 2018 FIFA World Cup Final.

Since the first one in 1982, there have been 26 penalty shoot-outs at the FIFA World Cup Finals.

Awesome awards

As well as the FIFA World Cup Trophy, other incredible awards are up for grabs at Russia 2018....

adidas Golden Ball
This is awarded to the player who has lit up the Finals more than any other. Argentina's Lionel Messi won it at Brazil 2014.

adidas Golden Boot
This trophy is given to the player who scores the most goals at the Finals. Colombia hero James Rodríguez scooped it in 2014.

adidas Golden Glove
Goalkeepers can also take some individual glory. The best keeper is given this award – at Brazil 2014 it was Germany's Manuel Neuer.

Every FIFA World Cup™ winner

1930	Uruguay	1966	England	1994	Brazil
1934	Italy	1970	Brazil	1998	France
1938	Italy	1974	West Germany	2002	Brazil
1950	Uruguay	1978	Argentina	2006	Italy
1954	West Germany	1982	Italy	2010	Spain
1958	Brazil	1986	Argentina	2014	Germany
1962	Brazil	1990	West Germany		

© FIFA TM

10 Top FIFA World Cup™ Facts

Do you want to brush up on your FIFA World Cup knowledge? Fancy impressing your friends and family with some fascinating football trivia? Check out these top ten facts, and remember to try the Russia 2018 quiz on pages 58-61!

Germany hero Miroslav Klose is his country's record scorer, with 71 goals.

1. Mega Mascot

The Russia 2018 mascot is a football-crazy grey wolf called Zabivaka. His name means "the one who scores" in Russian and the skilful hero will appear at all 64 games at the Finals!

© FIFA TM

2. FIFA Fan Fests

Thousands of supporters will watch the live action on giant screens at special FIFA Fan Fest areas in all 11 host cities. These exciting stages will also have music, performances, food and other fun activities.

3. Terrific Tour

Taken to 54 countries, more than 60 cities, covering 152,000 kilometres and seen by over one million fans, the FIFA World Cup Trophy Tour let supporters see the famous Trophy with their own eyes. Standing next to the Trophy and having your picture taken is epic!

4. Sweet 16

At Brazil 2014, Germany striker Miroslav Klose scored a record 16th FIFA World Cup Finals goal. Klose also played in the 2002, 2006 and 2010 tournaments.

5. Fab three

Brazil striker Pelé is the only player to win three FIFA World Cup winner's medals, in 1958, 1962 and 1970. Brazil star Cafu holds the record for appearing in the Final three times in a row, in 1994, 1998 and 2002.

Howard Webb shows a yellow card to the Netherlands' Robin van Persie in the 2010 Final.

6. Card crazy

At the 2010 World Cup Final between Spain and Netherlands, 14 yellow cards and one red were shown by English referee Howard Webb. That is more than in any other Final.

7. Ball blast

It will be tricky keeping count of all the adidas footballs at Russia 2018! An amazing 3,240 balls were used in matches and training at the 2014 Finals, and a similar number will be in use again this year.

Cafu celebrates with the FIFA World Cup Trophy in 2002, the last time that Brazil won the tournament.

8. Top tech

The first FIFA World Cup Finals goal to be awarded by goal-line technology was scored at Brazil 2014. Special cameras proved that a shot by France's Karim Benzema crept over the line against Honduras. More tech-driven goals could cause drama at Russia 2018.

9. Euro challenge

Only once has a country from outside Europe won a FIFA World Cup Finals in Europe. That was when Brazil became champions in Sweden in 1958. With the 2018 Final taking place in the European city of Moscow, perhaps a South American, Asian or African team will challenge their Euro rivals?

10. Brilliant Brazil

Nicknamed the Samba Boys, Brazil are the only nation to feature at every FIFA World Cup tournament. They have appeared in seven Finals, winning the Trophy on a record five occasions.

Super Stadium Guide

The 2018 FIFA World Cup™ will be played at 12 incredible stadiums in 11 host cities through the vast country of Russia. Eight new stadiums have been constructed since the Finals were awarded to Russia in 2010, two have been adapted from other sports, and two existing Moscow sites have been upgraded. Here, you can take a tour of all these amazing venues.

Rostov Arena

Capacity: 45,145
City: Rostov-on-Don
A slick new stadium built for the Finals, Rostov Arena sits on the banks of the River Don in the port of Rostov-on-Don. The stadium's innovative design sees the roof shape reflect the twists and turns of the river. FC Rostov will move into the arena after the Finals.

Kaliningrad Stadium

Capacity: 35,212
City: Kaliningrad
Built in the city of Kaliningrad, on Russia's beautiful west coast by the Baltic Sea, this brand-new, state-of-the-art stadium will host four group games. After the competition, Russian team FC Baltika Kaliningrad will play their home games here.

Spartak Stadium

Capacity: 43,298
City: Moscow
The hi-tech Spartak Stadium was opened in 2014. It is the home of the famous Spartak Moscow team and its outer skin is made up of thousands of diamond shapes, which change colour depending on the teams playing. Spartak Stadium will host four group games and one knockout game.

Saint Petersburg Stadium

Capacity: 68,134
City: Saint Petersburg
The second-largest stadium at the 2018 FIFA World Cup, the new Saint Petersburg Stadium will host seven games, including a semi-final. Designed to be one of the most modern venues in the world, it has a retractable roof and a sliding pitch, and its seven stories reach nearly 60 metres into the sky.

The Saint Petersburg stadium hosted the final of the 2017 FIFA Confederations Cup.

> The Fisht Stadium has been converted from an indoor arena to an open-air venue.

Fisht Stadium
Capacity: 47,700
City: Sochi
On the southwest coast of Russia, next to the Black Sea, the city of Sochi is a top tourist attraction. The Fisht Stadium was built for the 2014 Winter Olympics and has been altered for the tournament to boost capacity to over 47,000. It is named after Mount Fisht in the nearby Caucasus mountains.

Kazan Arena
Capacity: 44,779
City: Kazan
If the Kazan Arena looks familiar to English fans, that could be because it was built by the same people who designed Arsenal's Emirates Stadium and Wembley Stadium in London. Six FIFA World Cup games will be played at the venue.

Mordovia Arena
Capacity: 44,442
City: Saransk
Possibly the brightest stadium at the Finals, the Mordovia Arena is a crazy mix of orange, red and white to represent the traditional arts and craft designs of western Russia. After the FIFA World Cup, the oval-shaped arena will be home to FC Mordovia, and stage volleyball, basketball and tennis events.

Nizhny Novgorod Stadium
Capacity: 45,331
City: Nizhny Novgorod
Visitors to this stadium, which is situated near the Alexander Nevsky Cathedral and the Nizhny Novgorod Kremlin, will be able to take in the sights of this gorgeous city. The stadium was built especially for Russia 2018 and has a semi-transparent outer shell that pulls light into the arena.

Ekaterinburg Arena
Capacity: 35,696
City: Ekaterinburg
A stadium steeped in history from its origins in the 1950s, the Ekaterinburg Arena has been updated many times while still keeping its classic Soviet-style design at heart. A roof and temporary stands have been built to allow this pretty arena to stage four group games.

Samara Arena
Capacity: 44,807
City: Samara
The design of the new Samara Arena is out of this world – literally! Drawing on the Samara region's space travel heritage, the stadium resembles a giant glass dome with panels that light up at night. FC Krylya Sovetov are the lucky team who will play their home games at the stadium after the Finals.

Volgograd Arena
Capacity: 45,568
City: Volgograd
Volgograd, which used to be called Stalingrad, has a strong industrial heritage. This stadium looks both mechanical, like the spokes on a bicycle wheel, and artistic with its upside-down cone shape and open lattice design. The Volgograd Arena will be the venue for four games.

> The Luzhniki Stadium has hosted the Olympic Games and the UEFA Champions League final.

Luzhniki Stadium
Capacity: 81,006
City: Moscow
The huge Luzhniki Stadium in Russia's capital, Moscow, will be the venue for the host nation's opening game on 14 June. It will also stage one of the semi-finals and the Final on 15 July. The Luzhniki Stadium was originally opened in 1956 but has been thoroughly upgraded and refurbished for 2018.

Russia
Group A

As host nation and with their fans desperate to see Russia reach the knockout rounds, the pressure is on for the team to deliver on the big stage. Results have been mixed in Russia's friendly and competitive games, but draws in 2017 with Belgium and Chile gave them a lot of confidence. Much will be expected of the imposing strike force of Artem Dzyuba and Fyodor Smolov, who will be supplied by the experienced Yury Zhirkov and young talent of Aleksandr Golovin in midfield. Winning the opening game against Saudia Arabia on 14 June would set Russia up for an amazing tournament.

TEAM GUIDE
Captain: Igor Akinfeev
Coach: Stanislav Cherchesov
Route to Russia: Qualified automatically as hosts
Previous appearances: 10 (including as Soviet Union)
Best finish: Quarter-finals 1966 (as Soviet Union)

Players to watch
Igor Akinfeev: Hugely experienced goalkeeper
Aleksandr Golovin: Energetic, creative midfielder
Fyodor Smolov: Quality goal-grabber

Igor Akinfeev played all three of Russia's group games at Brazil 2014.

Aleksandr Golovin's first goal for Russia came just 16 minutes into his debut in June 2015.

100
Captain Igor Akinfeev made his 100th Russian appearance at the 2017 FIFA Confederations Cup.

Saudi Arabia
Group A

After failing to qualify for South Africa 2010 and Brazil 2014, Saudi Arabia put their faith in one man to finally return them to the FIFA World Cup™ Finals. Dutch coach Bert van Marwijk had guided the Netherlands to the 2010 Final and after taking charge of the Green Falcons in 2015, he oversaw 11 wins from 17 games to book a spot at Russia 2018. Edgardo Bauza is now the manager after Marwijk left in September 2017. Saudi Arabia like to play an attractive, attacking style with Mohammed Al-Sahlawi – who struck an incredible 16 goals on the way to Russia 2018 – as the focus.

TEAM GUIDE
Captain: Osama Hawsawi
Coach: Juan Antonio Pizzi
Route to Russia: Winners, AFC Group A round two; runners-up, Group B round three
Previous appearances: 4
Best finish: Second round 1994

Players to watch
Mohammed Al-Sahlawi: International goal machine
Taisir Al-Jassim: Attacking midfield threat
Yahya Al-Shehri: Skilful goalscoring winger

The experienced Mohammed Al-Sahlawi is ready to score his first FIFA World Cup Finals goal.

Yahya Al-Shehri scored a crucial winner against Iraq in qualifying for Russia 2018.

45
The number of goals Saudi Arabia scored in 18 FIFA World Cup qualifiers to reach Russia 2018.

Egypt
Group A

When Liverpool star Mohamed Salah scored a dramatic injury-time winner against Congo last October, it booked Egypt's first trip to the FIFA World Cup™ Finals since 1990. Héctor Cúper's team will need Salah, who bagged five goals in qualifying and is a free-kick and penalty expert, to be on top of his game in Russia. Egypt, though, are a well organised and patient team who like to use two defensive midfielders and launch quick-fire attacks. Their target in 2018 is to reach the knockout stage for the first time.

In 2017-18, defender Ahmed Hegazi impressed for West Bromwich Albion in the Premier League.

TEAM GUIDE
Captain: Essam El Hadary
Coach: Héctor Cúper
Route to Russia: Winners, CAF Group E round three
Previous appearances: 2
Best finish: Group stage 1990, 1934

Players to watch
Mohamed Salah: Goalscoring playmaker
Ramadan Sobhi: Eye-catching winger
Essam El Hadary: Superb shot-stopper

45
The age of goalkeeper Essam El Hadary, making him the oldest player at a FIFA World Cup Finals.

Mohamed Salah will be a big danger from the wings and in the penalty box.

Uruguay
Group A

Finishing second in the CONMEBOL qualifying group, ahead of 2014 FIFA World Cup™ runners-up Argentina, shows the quality coach Óscar Tabárez has in his Uruguay team. Experienced stars such as Luis Suárez, Edinson Cavani, Diego Godín and goalkeeper Fernando Muslera were in the squad that reached the semi-finals in 2010. Now with some fresh young players, most noticeably Real Madrid's all-action midfielder Federico Valverde, Uruguay may just cause a few shocks again in Russia. The strikeforce of Suárez and Cavani is one of the most lethal in international football and will give defenders a big headache.

TEAM GUIDE

Captain: Diego Godín
Coach: Óscar Tabárez
Route to Russia: Runners-up, CONMEBOL group
Previous appearances: 12
Best finish: Champions 1950, 1930

Players to watch
Luis Suárez: Penalty-box predator
Edinson Cavani: Powerful striker
Diego Godín: Defensive organizer

At South Africa 2010, Luis Suárez was shown a red card for handling the ball against Ghana.

Cavani plays club football for PSG in France, alongside Brazil hero Neymar.

5
The number of FIFA World Cup Finals goals scored by Luis Suárez. The Barcelona ace also has 21 in 48 qualifiers.

Portugal
Group B

Portugal may feel they have the perfect blend of experience and youth in their squad as they chase their first appearance in a FIFA World Cup™ Final. The star of the show, as always, is captain Cristiano Ronaldo. Portugal's record goalscorer struck 15 times in qualifying and he is joined by seasoned leaders Pepe, João Moutinho and Ricardo Quaresma. The team's exciting youth comes from players such as Renato Sanches and André Silva. Silva really caught the eye in qualifying with nine goals from ten games. The UEFA EURO 2016 champions will be well fancied to reach the knockout stage.

TEAM GUIDE
Captain: Cristiano Ronaldo
Coach: Fernando Santos
Route to Russia: Winners, UEFA Group B
Previous appearances: 6
Best finish: Third 1966

Players to watch
Cristiano Ronaldo: Mercurial goal king
André Silva: Young attacking ace
Pepe: Defensive lynchpin

In his club career Cristiano Ronaldo has won the UEFA Champions League, La Liga and Premier League titles.

AC Milan striker André Silva will be playing in his first FIFA World Cup Finals.

79
Cristiano Ronaldo's 15 qualifying goals took his tally for Portugal to 79 from 147 games.

Spain
Group B

Finishing ahead of Italy in UEFA Group G, and their impressive 3-0 demolition of the Italians in Madrid in September 2017, reminded everyone just how good the 2010 FIFA World Cup™ winners are. Key players from that victorious squad of eight years ago, such as David Silva, Sergio Ramos, Andrés Iniesta and Gerard Piqué, are chasing glory once again in Russia. Throw in Spain's awesome attacking talent of Isco, Álvaro Morata and Marco Asensio, and it is difficult to see any team stopping them from reaching at least the semi-finals this summer. Spain's second FIFA World Cup Finals victory this decade is well within the reach of coach Julen Lopetegui and his all-star squad.

TEAM GUIDE
Captain: Sergio Ramos
Coach: Julen Lopetegui
Route to Russia: Winners, UEFA Group G
Previous appearances: 14
Best finish: Champions 2010

Players to watch
Sergio Ramos: Inspirational captain and defender
David Silva: Controls the midfield
Isco: Goalscorer and creator

Isco was in fine form in qualifying, scoring two goals against Italy as Spain topped UEFA Group G.

Álvaro Morata scored five goals in qualifying, four of which came against Liechtenstein.

0
When Spain beat Italy 3-0 in FIFA World Cup qualifying, they started the game with no recognised striker in their line-up.

Morocco
Group B

After securing six clean sheets in a row in qualifying, it is clear that Morocco's strengths are in their defensive organisation. Their backline is built around Juventus defender Mehdi Benatia, who also scored an important goal against major qualifying rivals Ivory Coast last year. Khalid Boutaïb's stunning hat-trick knocked out Gabon and he is likely to spearhead Hervé Renard's attack as Morocco target the knockout stage for the first time in 32 years. After picking up 14 yellow cards and one red to reach Russia, the Atlas Lions will need to keep their cool under the spotlight this summer.

TEAM GUIDE

Captain: Mehdi Benatia
Coach: Hervé Renard
Route to Russia: Winners, CAF Group C round three
Previous appearances: 4
Best finish: Round of 16 1986

Players to watch

Mehdi Benatia: Strong in both boxes
Khalid Boutaïb: Big threat in the air
Hakim Ziyach: Free-kick and penalty expert

4

Coach Hervé Renard has managed four African nations – Morocco, Ivory Coast, Angola and Zambia (twice).

Mehdi Benatia will captain Morocco's first FIFA World Cup™ Finals team in 20 years.

Khalid Boutaïb scored six goals in his first 13 games for Morocco.

Iran
Group B

Built around a super-strong defence, Asian giants Iran will be a tough team to crack at Russia 2018. Undefeated in rounds two and three of their AFC qualifiers, they let in just five goals in 18 games. That strength in their backline is thanks to the organization from manager Carlos Queiroz, who used to coach at Real Madrid and Manchester United, and the experience of key defenders such as Ramin Rezaeian and Morteza Pouraliganji. In attack Iran rely on the net-bulging talent of Mehdi Taremi and Sardar Azmoun, and the sparkle from Alireza Jahanbakhsh's boots on the wings. At the 2018 Finals, Iran's goal is to reach the round of 16 for the first time.

TEAM GUIDE

Captain: Ashkan Dejagah
Coach: Carlos Queiroz
Route to Russia: Winners, AFC Group D round two; winners, Group A round three
Previous appearances: 4
Best finish: Group stage 2014, 2006, 1998, 1978

Players to watch
Alireza Jahanbakhsh: Silky midfield skills
Mehdi Taremi: Dangerous goalscorer
Ramin Rezaeian: Attacking right-back

Winger Alireza Jahanbakhsh is one of the most exciting players in the Dutch Eredivisie.

Sardar Azmoun has been called the 'Iranian Messi' thanks to his goals and assists.

12
In August 2017, Iran set a FIFA World Cup qualifying record of 12 clean sheets in a row.

France
Group C

It was 20 years ago when France first won the FIFA World Cup™. They reached the final in 2006 too, only to lose a dramatic penalty shoot-out to Italy, and in 2018 they are dreaming of winning the famous golden Trophy for a second time. This year they have the goals of Antoine Griezmann, the midfield power of Paul Pogba and the pace and precision of Kylian Mbappé in attack. Coach Didier Deschamps was the man who captained France to that famous win in Paris in 1998. With him in charge, French dreams could become a reality in Russia this summer.

TEAM GUIDE
Captain: Hugo Lloris
Coach: Didier Deschamps
Route to Russia: Winners, UEFA Group A
Previous appearances: 14
Best finish: Champions 1998

Players to watch
Antoine Griezmann: Penalty-box predator
Paul Pogba: Midfield dynamo
Kylian Mbappé: Quick and skilful forward

Antoine Griezmann was the top scorer at UEFA EURO 2016, with six goals.

Kylian Mbappé scored his first goal for France in a 4-0 qualifying win over the Netherlands in August 2017.

70
Hugo Lloris has captained France more times than any other player. He has been captain for 70 of his 94 games.

Australia
Group C

Australia's 22-game route to reach the 2018 FIFA World Cup™ Finals began in June 2015 and finally ended in November 2017 with a 3-1 play-off win over Honduras. Tim Cahill, Mile Jedinak and Tom Rogic grabbed the headlines thanks to their qualifying goals, but the Socceroos have a fantastic spirit and strong work ethic that may see them surprise a few teams in Russia. Australia's midfield sparkles with the set-piece skills of Aaron Mooy and the mercurial talent of Massimo Luongo. And will the long-serving Cahill join legends such as Pelé and Miroslav Klose in scoring at four Finals?

TEAM GUIDE
Captain: Mile Jedinak
Coach: Not yet confirmed
Route to Russia: Winners, AFC Group B round two; third place, Group B round three; play-offs
Previous appearances: 4
Best finish: Round of 16 2006

Players to watch
Tim Cahill: Goal hero at the Finals
Mile Jedinak: Controls the midfield
Aaron Mooy: Ace free-kicks and corners

Midfielder Aaron Mooy has been in top form for Huddersfield Town in the Premier League.

Tim Cahill will be 38 years old at the Finals, but his experience will be vital for the Socceroos.

5
Tim Cahill has an eventful Finals record, scoring five goals in eight matches but also collecting four yellow cards and one red.

Peru
Group C

Peru battled through to Russia 2018 after beating New Zealand in a tense play-off, but Ricardo Gareca's entertaining team are well worth their place. In the CONMEBOL qualifying group Peru scored more goals than Argentina and in October 2017 they reached the top ten of the FIFA/Coca-Cola World Rankings for the first time. With exciting wingers such as André Carrillo and Edison Flores and a 4-2-3-1 system that can launch fast counter attacks, Peru are another stylish South American side confident of winning games at the 2018 FIFA World Cup™.

TEAM GUIDE

Captain: Alberto Rodriguez
Coach: Ricardo Gareca
Route to Russia: Fifth, CONMEBOL group; play-offs
Previous appearances: 4
Best finish: Quarter-finals 1970

Players to watch
Jefferson Farfán: Fast, powerful striker
Christian Cueva: Bursts into the box
Yoshimar Yotún: Top tackler and passer

36
The number of years since Peru last played at a FIFA World Cup Finals.

Striker Jefferson Farfán scored a crucial goal in Peru's 2-0 play-off win against New Zealand.

Attacking midfielder Christian Cueva is Peru's key goal maker.

Denmark
Group C

The great Danes booked their spot at Russia 2018 in fantastic style. Their 5-1 second-leg play-off win over Republic of Ireland shows how deadly Denmark can be, especially when Christian Eriksen has his goalscoring boots on. The Tottenham trickster blasted a hat-trick in that game and his runs into the box and fierce free-kicks will be his country's main weapon this summer. Watch out too for emerging Bundesliga star Thomas Delaney – he sparked into life at the end of the qualifying campaign with four goals and some impressive displays.

TEAM GUIDE

Captain: Simon Kjaer
Coach: Åge Hareide
Route to Russia: Runners-up, UEFA Group E; play-offs
Previous appearances: 4
Best finish: Quarter-finals 1998

Players to watch
Christian Eriksen: Skilful and full of goals
Thomas Delaney: Dangerous attacking midfielder
Kasper Schmeichel: Commanding goalkeeper

Christian Eriksen is a goal creator too, and had three assists in qualifying.

Kasper Schmeichel's father, Peter, played in Denmark's run to the 1998 FIFA World Cup™ quarter-finals.

11

With 11 goals, Christian Eriksen was the top-scoring midfielder among all European teams in qualifying.

Argentina
Group D

Given the world-class stars Argentina have, and the fact they were FIFA World Cup™ runners-up in 2014, it is incredible that they needed to win their final qualifier to reach Russia. The saviour, once again, was Lionel Messi. He scored a hat-trick to take Argentina to their 17th Finals and now the Barcelona superstar is looking to improve on his return of five goals in 15 Finals games. Messi will be backed by tantalizing attackers such as Sergio Agüero, Gonzalo Higuaín and Ángel di María as Argentina battle for their third world title this summer.

Gonzalo Higuaín scored a hat-trick against South Korea at the 2010 FIFA World Cup.

7
Argentina's famous number ten, Lionel Messi, scored seven qualifying goals in just ten matches.

Lionel Messi will be appearing at his fourth FIFA World Cup Finals.

Iceland
Group D

Iceland were 'ice cool' in qualifying for Russia 2018, which is their first FIFA World Cup™ Finals. After surprisingly reaching the quarter-finals of UEFA EURO 2016, Iceland impressed again by topping Group I and are a team that no country will relish taking on. They kept five clean sheets in qualifying and when playmaker Gylfi Sigurðsson gets the ball, he has the talent to pick a perfect pass or test the keeper with a long-range strike. Watch out, too, for the Iceland players and fans performing their famous Viking thunderclap celebration!

TEAM GUIDE
Captain: Aron Gunnarsson
Coach: Heimir Hallgrímsson
Route to Russia: Winners, UEFA Group I
Previous appearances: 0

Players to watch
Gylfi Sigurðsson: Creative midfielder, set-piece star
Alfreð Finnbogason: Dangerous in the box
Jóhann Guðmundsson: Hardworking winger

Tough-tackling midfielder Aron Gunnarsson will protect Iceland's defence.

Gylfi Sigurðsson was Iceland's top scorer in qualifying with four goals.

335,000
The population of Iceland. They are the smallest nation to reach a FIFA World Cup Finals.

Croatia
Group D

Luka Modrić was only 12 years old when Croatia surprisingly reached the semi-finals of the 1998 FIFA World Cup™, and now 20 years later the Real Madrid star captains his country for the first time at the Finals. He forms a strong midfield partnership with Barcelona ace Ivan Rakitić, while Juventus forward Mario Mandžukić leads a fierce attack. Croatia conceded just four goals in their qualifying group and breezed past Greece 4-1 on aggregate in the play-offs. New coach Zlatko Dalić, who only took charge in October, has made them very tough to beat.

TEAM GUIDE
Captain: Luka Modrić
Coach: Zlatko Dalić
Route to Russia: Runners-up, UEFA Group I; play-offs
Previous appearances: 4
Best finish: Third place 1998

Players to watch
Luka Modrić: Midfield master
Ivan Rakitić: Energy, skill and goals
Mario Mandžukić: Strong penalty-box predator

Mario Mandžukić is Croatia's second-highest goalscorer, with 30 goals in 80 games.

35
Striker Mario Mandžukić scored a hat-trick in just 35 minutes against Kosovo in qualifying.

Luka Modrić reached the quarter-finals of UEFA EURO 2008 with Croatia.

Nigeria
Group D

Nigeria could be the most dangerous African team at the FIFA World Cup™. Coach Gernot Rohr has experienced stars who have played at the Finals before, plus exciting youngsters ready to make a name. The displays of powerful midfielder John Obi Mikel and goals from winger Victor Moses will be important. Watch out too for exciting 21-year-old Kelechi Iheanacho, who scored when Nigeria won the FIFA Under-17 World Cup in 2013. Leicester City forward Ahmed Musa netted twice against Argentina at Brazil 2014 and is a potent weapon either as a starter or from the bench. The Super Eagles are out to have a super time in Russia!

TEAM GUIDE

Captain: John Obi Mikel
Coach: Gernot Rohr
Route to Russia: Winners, CAF Group B round three
Previous appearances: 5
Best finish: Round of 16 2014, 1998, 1994

Players to watch
Victor Moses: Speedy attacking skills
John Obi Mikel : Tricky midfield attacker
Kelechi Iheanacho: Dangerous in the box

Ahmed Musa loves to dribble the ball and take shots from outside the box.

John Obi Mikel played his first senior game for Nigeria in 2005.

5

In 1994 Nigeria reached fifth place in the FIFA World Rankings, which is the highest ever position by an African nation.

29

Brazil
Group E

When coach Tite took charge in 2016, Brazil were struggling to even make it to the Finals. The five-time champions then won their next nine qualifiers to reach Russia 2018 in style, with goalscorers Neymar, Philippe Coutinho and Gabriel Jesus in fine form. Predictably, Brazil have plenty of options in attack but it is their defensive power that gives them the confidence to win every game. Marquinhos, Dani Alves and Miranda have made the backline into a brick wall and, in front of them, midfielder Paulinho is both a goal stopper and scorer. Despite dramatically crashing out in the semi-finals in 2014, Brazil will be the team to beat once again.

TEAM GUIDE

Captain: Not yet confirmed
Coach: Tite
Route to Russia: Winners, CONMEBOL group
Previous appearances: 20
Best finish: Champions 2002, 1994, 1970, 1962, 1958

Players to watch

Neymar: Spectacular goalscorer
Paulinho: All-action midfielder
Philippe Coutinho: Attacking flair

Paulinho scored a hat-trick in a 4-1 win over Uruguay in qualifying.

Midfielder Philippe Coutinho scored in Brazil's 3-0 win over Paraguay that secured qualification.

41

Brazil blasted 41 goals in qualifying for Russia 2018, winning nine games in a row.

Switzerland
Group E

A 2-0 loss to Portugal in their final qualifier put Switzerland into a tense play-off with Northern Ireland, but their impressive defence helped them make it through to Russia. Vladimir Petković's hardworking team kept five clean sheets in a row in qualifying and actually beat UEFA EURO 2016 champions Portugal in their first meeting. Switzerland will need Haris Seferović and Xherdan Shaqiri to both score and create goals. At the 2014 FIFA World Cup™, winger Shaqiri bagged a hat-trick against Honduras and could catch the eye again this summer with his slick skills.

TEAM GUIDE
Captain: Stephan Lichtsteiner
Coach: Vladimir Petković
Route to Russia: Runners-up, UEFA Group B; play-offs
Previous appearances: 10
Best finish: Quarter-finals 1954, 1938, 1934

Players to watch
Ricardo Rodríguez: Goalscoring defender
Xherdan Shaqiri: Quick-footed midfielder
Granit Xhaka: Links defence and midfield

Haris Seferović played at the 2014 FIFA World Cup and at UEFA EURO 2016.

Stoke City's Xherdan Shaqiri has also starred for Bayern Munich and Inter Milan.

14
An amazing 14 different players scored for Switzerland during qualifying.

Costa Rica
Group E

Can Costa Rica be a surprise team in Russia? At Brazil 2014, Los Ticos topped their group ahead of Uruguay, Italy and England and came within a penalty shoot-out of reaching the semi-finals. The stars of that tournament, such as Bryan Ruiz, Celso Borges, Joel Campbell and goalkeeper Keylor Navas, took Costa Rica to another Finals with a game to spare. Their midfield is creative and combative, with Ruiz and Campbell clocking up five goals in qualifying, while key centre-back Giancarlo González works hard to protect his goal.

In 2017 Keylor Navas won the UEFA Champions League and La Liga with Real Madrid.

Bryan Ruiz has 14 goals in FIFA World Cup Finals and qualifying games.

100
Captain Bryan Ruiz played his 100th game for Costa Rica last July.

Serbia
Group E

With just one defeat in qualifying, Serbia are aiming to make up for missing the 2014 Finals by reaching the knockout stages in Russia. While not all of their players are well-known stars, the Serbia midfield is led by Manchester United's Nemanja Matić and Southampton's Dušan Tadić. Tadić has been in top form for his country, scoring four goals in ten qualifiers. He was named Serbian Player of the Year in 2016 and has all the skills needed to wear his country's playmaker number ten shirt. With veterans Branislav Ivanovic and Aleksandar Kolarov in defence, Serbia will be tough to break down in Russia.

TEAM GUIDE
Captain: Branislav Ivanovic
Coach: Not yet confirmed
Route to Russia: Winners, UEFA Group D
Previous appearances: 11
Best finish: Fourth place 1962, 1930 (as Yugoslavia)

Players to watch
Dušan Tadić: Goalscorer and creator
Nemanja Matić: Experienced midfielder
Aleksandar Kolarov: Attack-minded defender

Aleksandar Mitrovic struck an impressive six goals in just nine qualifying games.

Attacking midfielder Dušan Tadić has played over 100 Premier League games for Southampton.

1
The number of qualifying goals Aleksandar Prijović scored – but his strike was a crucial winner against Georgia.

Germany
Group F

The reigning FIFA World Cup™ champions go to Russia with an impressive qualifying campaign behind them. World-class talent such as Thomas Müller and Mesut Özil crushed Norway, Czech Republic and Northern Ireland as they stormed to their 17th FIFA World Cup tournament in a row. Germany are the only country to appear in eight Finals, winning four of them, and only once have they failed to reach the last eight. The team is based on a rock-solid defence led by Bayern Munich keeper Manuel Neuer, and bristles with goal potential thanks to Müller, Özil, Mario Gómez, Toni Kroos, André Schürrle and Mario Götze.

Midfielder Toni Kroos completed 537 passes at Brazil 2014, the second highest number behind team-mate Philipp Lahm.

Can Manuel Neuer repeat his adidas Golden Glove win from Brazil 2014?

224
That's how many FIFA World Cup finals goals Germany have scored – three more than Brazil.

Mexico
Group F

Making their seventh FIFA World Cup™ Finals appearance in a row, Mexico go to Russia 2018 dreaming of repeating their quarter-final run of 1986. Qualifying with three games to spare shows the quality and attacking talent the team has. Coach Juan Carlos Osorio has an organised defence, marshaled by Diego Antonio Reyes, and relies on the midfield power of Andrés Guardado and trickery of Hirving Lozano. The experienced Javier Hernández, who can play in midfield and attack, will link up with Carlos Vela, who scored three times in qualifying and is ready to hit his first FIFA World Cup Finals goals.

TEAM GUIDE

Captain: Andrés Guardado
Coach: Juan Carlos Osorio
Route to Russia: Winners, CONCACAF round five
Previous appearances: 15
Best finish: Quarter-finals 1986

Players to watch
Javier Hernández: Versatile goal poacher
Carlos Vela: Lethal left-footed attacker
Andrés Guardado: Midfield pass master

Andrés Guardado has over 140 Mexico caps and has played at three FIFA World Cups.

6
Mexico have reached the last 16 stage of the previous six FIFA World Cups.

Star striker Javier Hernández has scored 11 goals in FIFA World Cup Finals games and qualifiers.

Sweden
Group F

"An unbelievable joy," is how Sweden captain Andreas Granqvist described reaching Russia 2018. His team caused the biggest upset in the play-offs as they beat Italy 1-0 over two legs. Without the retired Zlatan Ibrahimović, Marcus Berg has the job of finding the net this summer with help from attacking talent such as Ola Toivonen, Emil Forsberg and Sebastian Larsson. Sweden have a fine history at the FIFA World Cup™ Finals and if they play to their counter-attacking strengths they may well create a few shocks again.

TEAM GUIDE
Captain: Andreas Granqvist
Coach: Janne Andersson
Route to Russia: Runners-up, UEFA Group A; play-offs
Previous appearances: 11
Best finish: Runners-up 1958
Players to watch
Marcus Berg: Alert in the box
Victor Lindelöf: Tough Manchester United defender
Sebastian Larsson: Experienced free-kick master

Marcus Berg struck four goals in an 8-0 qualifying win over Luxembourg.

Sebastian Larsson has played at three UEFA EUROs but Russia 2018 is his first FIFA World Cup Finals.

8
Striker Marcus Berg was Sweden's top scorer in qualifying with eight goals.

Korea Republic
Group F

Although Korea Republic are now FIFA World Cup™ regulars, matching heavyweights such as Spain, Italy and Germany by reaching every tournament since 1986, the Taeguk Warriors had a bumpy journey to Russia. Their final two qualifiers were goalless draws with Uzbekistan and Iran, and key forward Son Heung-min, who plays for Tottenham, needs to make an impact in Russia if Korea are to make it out of their group. Veteran striker Lee Dong-gook played for Korea at France 1998 and it would be quite a story if he appeared at the Finals 20 years later.

TEAM GUIDE

Captain: Ki Sung-yueng
Coach: Shin Tae-yong
Route to Russia: Winners, AFC Group G round two; runners-up, Group A round three
Previous appearances: 9
Best finish: Semi-finals 2002

Players to watch
Son Heung-min: Versatile attacker
Ki Sung-yueng: Experienced midfield leader
Kim Young-gwon: Powerful centre-back

Son Heung-min has an impressive record of eight goals in 22 FIFA World Cup qualifiers.

Ki Sung-yueng become Korea's captain after Park Ji-sung retired in 2014.

9
Korea Republic will be appearing in their ninth FIFA World Cup tournament in a row.

Belgium
Group G

With world-class players such as Eden Hazard, Romelu Lukaku and Kevin De Bruyne, it should be no surprise that Belgium are expected to have their best ever FIFA World Cup™ Finals this year. Under coach Roberto Martínez, the Red Devils scored 43 goals in qualifying, the joint highest in all nine UEFA groups, and have an experienced defence guided by Vincent Kompany, Toby Alderweireld and Jan Vertonghen. Many of the current squad reached the last eight at UEFA EURO 2016 and they will use that experience to target a place in the final four in Russia. Entertaining and exciting – keep your eyes on the boys from Belgium.

Midfielder Kevin De Bruyne helped Belgium reach the quarter-finals of both Brazil 2014 and EURO 2016.

Romelu Lukaku was in goal-hungry form during qualification, scoring 11 goals in just eight games.

21
Free-scoring Belgium bagged an impressive 21 goals in their first four qualifying games for Russia 2018.

Panama
Group G

Defender Román Torres was Panama's hero in his country's battle to reach their first FIFA World Cup™. His dramatic late winner against Costa Rica in their final qualifier booked their spot in Russia and Hernán Darío Gómez's team now take that momentum into the group games. Panama have plenty of experience in their squad, with Gabriel Gómez, Blas Pérez and Luis Tejada having over 100 caps each, while coach Gomez took Colombia and Ecuador to the FIFA World Cup in 1998 and 2002 respectively. Los Canaleros have their eyes on reaching the last 16.

TEAM GUIDE
Captain: Felipe Baloy
Coach: Hernán Darío Gómez
Route to Russia: Third, CONCACAF round five
Previous appearances: 0

Players to watch
Luis Tejada: Hugely experienced striker
Gabriel Torres: Pacey goal-getter
Jaime Penedo: Commanding goalkeeper

Blas Pérez will be 37 years old when Costa Rica begin their campaign in Russia.

Both of Luis Tejada's qualifying goals for Russia 2018 were against Costa Rica.

80
Luis Tejada and Blas Pérez have scored over 80 international goals between them.

Tunisia
Group G

Any nation that faces Tunisia in Russia and thinks they will have an easy game should look again at their results in qualifying. The Eagles of Carthage were undefeated in eight games and when they needed just a draw with Libya to book their spot at the Finals, Nabil Maaloul's team produced a fine defensive display. Youssef Msakni will love to show off his attacking skills on the biggest stage, while talented midfielder Ghilane Chaalani has become an eye-catching star in the white and red of Tunisia. Confidence is high and a place in the knockout stage is their target.

TEAM GUIDE

Captain: Aymen Mathlouthi
Coach: Nabil Maaloul
Route to Russia: Winners, CAF Group A round three
Previous appearances: 4
Best finish: Group stage 2006, 2002, 1998, 1978

Players to watch
Wahbi Khazri: Important goals and assists
Youssef Msakni: Exciting dribbler
Aymen Abdennour: Leads Tunisia's defence

Forward Youssef Msakni struck a hat-trick against Guinea to put Tunisia within reach of Russia 2018.

Tunisia number ten Wahbi Khazri will be the team's creative force.

1978

In 1978 Tunisia became the first African country to win a game at a FIFA World Cup Finals. They beat Mexico 3-1.

England
Group G

England have qualified for every FIFA World Cup™ Finals since 1998. Coach Gareth Southgate has a tough job to take them past the quarter-finals though, because that has not happened since 1990. With attacking talent such as Harry Kane and Jamie Vardy, backed up by the pace of Marcus Rashford, Raheem Sterling and Kyle Walker, England should create plenty of goalscoring chances. Tottenham star Dele Alli is the creative midfield force. England fans hope he will have a terrific first FIFA World Cup, just like Tottenham's Paul Gascoigne did back in 1990.

TEAM GUIDE
Captain: Not yet confirmed
Coach: Gareth Southgate
Route to Russia: Winners, UEFA Group F
Previous appearances: 14
Best finish: Champions 1966

Players to watch
Harry Kane: World-class striker
Dele Alli: Tricky midfield attacker
Marcus Rashford: Speedy striker or winger

Harry Kane scored in four of England's final five qualifiers for Russia 2018.

Marcus Rashford scored his first FIFA World Cup qualifying goal in September 2017.

1966
The only time England have won the FIFA World Cup, and appeared in the Final, was at Wembley in 1966.

41

Poland
Group H

Making their first FIFA World Cup™ Finals appearance since 2006, Poland are aiming to have a big impact – just like the teams of 1974 and 1982 that reached the semi-final stage. Lethal Bayern Munich striker Robert Lewandowski is the main man in attack and he can score goals from inside and outside the box. His link-up with the hardworking Arkadiusz Milik will threaten defences in Group H, and so will the super skills of wingers Kamil Grosicki and Jakub Błaszczykowski. After narrowly losing to Cristiano Ronaldo's Portugal in the last eight of UEFA EURO 2016, Poland want to go even further in Russia.

TEAM GUIDE

Captain: Robert Lewandowski
Coach: Adam Nawalka
Route to Russia: Winners, UEFA Group E
Previous appearances: 7
Best finish: Third place 1982, 1974

Players to watch
Robert Lewandowski: Brilliant target man
Kamil Glik: Tough-tackling centre-back
Arkadiusz Milik: Attacking flair

Lewandowski will be playing in his first FIFA World Cup Finals.

Kamil Grosicki was a key player in Poland's run to the quarter-finals of UEFA EURO 2016.

16
Robert Lewandowski hit a European record of 16 goals in qualifying, including two hat-tricks.

Senegal
Group H

Senegal have not been to a FIFA World Cup™ for 16 years, but coach Aliou Cissé knows all about glory at the Finals. He was the Senegal captain at Korea/Japan 2002 and helped create headlines as they stormed to the quarter-finals. With firepower from Sadio Mané, Diafra Sakho and Moussa Sow, the Lions of Teranga may upset more established nations once again in Russia. Many of the squad's big names star in the Premier League and Ligue 1, and that experience will be vital in the pressure-packed atmosphere of the world's biggest competition. Senegal want to celebrate again just like they did in Cissé's playing days.

TEAM GUIDE
Captain: Cheikhou Kouyaté
Coach: Aliou Cissé
Route to Russia: Winners, CAF Group D round three
Previous appearances: 1
Best finish: Quarter-finals 2002

Players to watch
Sadio Mané: Speedy winger or striker
Cheikhou Kouyaté: Keeps midfield ticking
Diafra Sakho: Energetic forward

Opposing defenders will watch Liverpool's skilful attacker Sadio Mané very closely.

Cheikhou Kouyaté reached the quarter-finals of the 2012 Olympic Games with Senegal.

2
Senegal scored two or more goals in seven of their eight qualifying games.

Colombia
Group H

Colombia go to Russia 2018, their second successive FIFA World Cup™ Finals and sixth in total, with memories of their amazing run to the quarter-finals four years ago still fresh in their minds. José Pékerman was the man in charge then and his clever leadership has worked magic again. Colombia's world-class strike duo of James Rodríguez and Radamel Falcao have the talent and finishing skills to worry any defence. For Falcao, in particular, these Finals are a pivotal tournament as he agonizingly missed Brazil 2014 through injury.

TEAM GUIDE
Captain: Radamel Falcao
Coach: José Pékerman
Route to Russia: Fourth, CONMEBOL group
Previous appearances: 5
Best finish: Quarter-finals 2014

Players to watch
James Rodríguez: Potent attacking midfielder
Radamel Falcao: Legendary goalscorer
David Ospina: Super-quick goalkeeping reflexes

James Rodríguez will be hoping to win back-to-back adidas Golden Boots.

In 2017 Radamel Falcao became Colombia's all-time top scorer.

6
James Rodríguez scored six goals in qualifying for Russia and six at Brazil 2014, when he won the adidas Golden Boot.

Japan
Group H

With stars such as Makoto Hasebe, Shinji Kagawa, Shinji Okazaki and Maya Yoshida playing in Europe's top leagues, Japan have the talent to reach the knockout stage for only the third time. Captain Hasebe anchors the midfield and with the former AC Milan playmaker Keisuke Honda still shining for the Samurai Blue, speedy striker Okazaki should have plenty of chances to add to his two FIFA World Cup™ Finals goals. Watch out too for striker Takuma Asano. Signed by Arsenal in 2016, the youngster has an eye for goal and could make a name for himself from the substitute's bench.

TEAM GUIDE

Captain: Makoto Hasebe
Coach: Vahid Halilhodzic
Route to Russia: Winners, AFC Group E round two; winners, Group B round three
Previous appearances: 5
Best finish: Round of 16 2010, 2002

Players to watch
Shinji Okazaki: Hard-working attacker
Keisuke Honda: Clever goal creator
Takuma Asano: Energetic striker

Centre-back Maya Yoshida played in all 18 of Japan's qualifiers.

Shinji Okazaki scored his 50th goal for Japan against Thailand in March 2017.

7

Japan conceded just seven goals in 18 FIFA World Cup qualifiers for Russia 2018.

FIFA World Cup™ Stars
Forwards

Thomas Müller

Country: Germany
Club: Bayern Munich (Germany)
Born: 13 September 1989

89 GAMES | 37 GOALS

Top skills: It is no surprise that Thomas Müller is a vital part of Germany's successful team. He can play as an attacking midfielder, on the wing or as a central striker and he is an invaluable source of goals for the reigning champions. Less of a dribbler and trickster than the likes of Neymar and Lionel Messi, Müller still shines for his country and has a terrific work rate. His understanding with Mario Götze, Mesut Özil and Julian Draxler means he will always be a superstar for Germany, as shown by his five goals in nine qualifiers for Russia 2018.

Romelu Lukaku

Country: Belgium
Club: Manchester United (England)
Born: 13 May 1993

63 GAMES | 28 GOALS

Top skills: Only Robert Lewandowski and Cristiano Ronaldo struck more goals than Lukaku in European qualifying for Russia 2018. The Belgian tucked away 11 in eight games and now his challenge is to add to his solitary strike from Brazil 2014. The Manchester United ace will be confident of that after a fine season in the Premier League. Not only does he have the power to dominate defenders, but he has a clever touch too as he links up with Eden Hazard and Kevin de Bruyne in the final third. Lukaku is a definite candidate for the adidas Golden Boot top scorer prize.

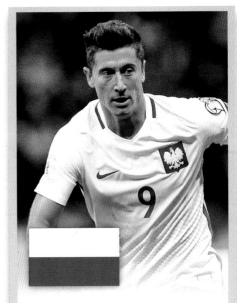

Robert Lewandowski

Country: Poland
Club: Bayern Munich (Germany)
Born: 21 August 1988

91 GAMES | 51 GOALS

Top skills: If a record of 16 goals from ten qualifiers is not frightening enough for defenders at Russia 2018, a close-up look at Robert Lewandowski's skills will be. The Poland captain is a world-class finisher who scores every type of goal, from precision headers to long-range blockbusters and laser-guided penalties. The Bayern Munich hero now has the chance to finally perform at a FIFA World Cup Finals, and Poland's chances of reaching the knockout stages rest largely on Lewandowski's shoulders. Stopping this legendary number 9 will not be easy.

Neymar

Country: Brazil
Club: Paris Saint-Germain (France)
Born: 5 February 1992

81 GAMES

52 GOALS

Top skills: Neymar is the star striker and talisman of the Brazil team. The fearsome forward has the speed, skill and deceptive strength to beat the world's best defenders and has an impressive record of four goals from his five FIFA World Cup Finals appearances. Neymar has lived up to the hype of becoming the world's most expensive player, after Paris Saint-Germain paid Barcelona €222 million for him in 2017, and he has been a sensation in the French league and UEFA Champions League. With Brazil, his attacking team-mates Philippe Coutinho, Gabriel Jesus and Roberto Firmino help him bang in the goals and beat goalkeepers from all angles. Neymar bagged six times as Brazil stormed through their qualifiers.

50

Neymar scored his 50th international goal as Brazil beat rivals Argentina in November 2016.

FIFA World Cup™ Stars Forwards

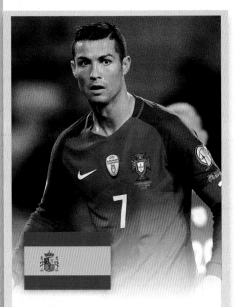

Cristiano Ronaldo

Country: Portugal
Club: Real Madrid (Spain)
Born: 5 February 1985

147 GAMES — 79 GOALS

Top skills: Cristiano Ronaldo has transformed from a tricky right winger into the most feared striker in world football. He has the speed, power, skills and vision to score big goals in big games – he has won the UEFA EUROs, UEFA Champions League, La Liga, Premier League and FIFA Club World Cup in his awesome career. Ronaldo shoots with either foot and is remarkably accurate with headers. Portugal's talisman has yet to really shine at a FIFA World Cup, scoring a modest three goals in 13 games, but his record of 30 goals in 38 qualifiers shows just how deadly he is.

Luis Suárez

Country: Uruguay
Club: Barcelona (Spain)
Born: 24 January 1987

95 GAMES — 49 GOALS

Top skills: Uruguay's record goalscorer is like a machine when he enters the area – if the ball is at his feet, it is pretty much guaranteed to be hitting the net a few seconds later! Suárez is super accurate with shooting and can tease and trick his way past defenders thanks to his clever close control. The striker is a real team player as well, with seven assists to add to his five goals in qualifying for Russia 2018. He also recorded five goals in eight games in total at the 2010 and 2014 FIFA World Cup Finals – this year he'll want to double that number.

Harry Kane

Country: England
Club: Tottenham (England)
Born: 28 July 1993

23 GAMES — 12 GOALS

Top skills: With five goals from just six Russia 2018 qualifying games, England fans came to rely on Harry Kane's blistering form around the opposition's penalty box. Kane, who is already a multiple Premier League Golden Boot winner, scored some important goals to reach the Finals, including a dramatic late leveler against Scotland and an injury-time winner over Slovenia. He has power, pace and the skill to blast or bend the ball with either foot from distance. On form, Kane is lethal with a strike partner and supporting wide players.

Lionel Messi

Country: Argentina
Club: Barcelona (Spain)
Born: 24 June 1987

122 GAMES

61 GOALS

Top skills: One of the most famous players on the planet and maybe the best of all time, Messi's magical skills are truly out of this world. He can play in any attacking position and with his sharp brain and lethal left foot, Messi loves to burst into the penalty area and bend, blast or roll the ball past the mesmerised keeper. Despite being small, Messi has no fear against tough defenders and will dribble his way into dangerous positions. Alongside attackers such as Sergio Agüero, Ángel di María and Gonzalo Higuaín, he can be unstoppable.

61

Messi is Argentina's top scorer of all time, with 61 international goals by the end of October 2017.

FIFA World Cup™ Stars
Midfielders

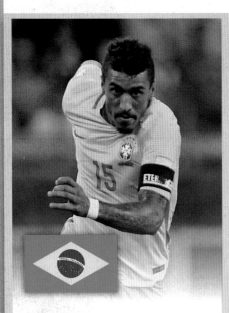

Paulinho

Country: Brazil
Club: Barcelona (Spain)
Born: 25 July 1988

45 GAMES **11 GOALS**

Top skills: Paulinho does not have the superstar profile of Neymar, but he is just as vital for Brazil. The all-action midfielder played in eight of the team's record nine qualifying wins in a row as they topped the South American CONMEBOL group. His hat-trick in Uruguay and strike against Argentina were particular highlights. After moving from Tottenham to China's Guangzhou Evergrande in 2015, Paulinho developed a sharp eye for goal. Since joining Barcelona in 2017 he has continued to shine with Lionel Messi and Luis Suárez in front of him.

Isco

Country: Spain
Club: Real Madrid (Spain)
Born: 21 April 1992

24 GAMES **7 GOALS**

Top skills: Francisco Roman Alarcon, better known as Isco, can hardly be called Spain's secret weapon at Russia 2018. The silky-skilled midfielder has been playing for his national team since 2013 and scored his first senior international goal in 2014. But it was Isco's performance in a 3-0 qualifying win over Italy in September 2017 that made him a hero. His two goals, including a fabulous free kick, set Spain on their way to Russia and cemented his spot in coach Julen Lopetegui's team. This summer Isco is ready to show the world just how good he is.

Paul Pogba

Country: France
Club: Manchester United (England)
Born: 15 March 1993

49 GAMES **8 GOALS**

Top skills: Pogba is perhaps Europe's most complete midfielder. The France icon has never-ending energy, amazingly slick skills and the height and power to dominate any opponent. The playmaker made headlines after a then-world-record move to Manchester United in 2016, shortly after the pain of playing for France in their UEFA EURO 2016 Final defeat to Portugal. Two years on from that game, and four years since he was named Hyundai Young Player at Brazil 2014, Pogba has his eyes on leading France to their third FIFA World Cup Final.

Eden Hazard

Country: Belgium
Club: Chelsea (England)
Born: 7 January 1991

81 GAMES · 20 GOALS

Top skills: Even though he is joined by superstars Kevin de Bruyne, Romelu Lukaku and Marouane Fellaini for Belgium, Eden Hazard is still the player that makes them tick. He makes them win too, steering the Red Devils to victories in all eight of the qualifiers in which he played. Hazard is a nightmare for defenders to mark as he drifts around the pitch, ghosting between midfield and attack and setting up chances. If he turns on the style, as he does so often in the Premier League and UEFA Champions League for Chelsea, Belgium could go a long way in Russia.

2016

In this year, Eden Hazard played his first senior international alongside his younger brother Thorgan.

51

FIFA World Cup™ Stars
Midfielders

Mesut Özil

Country: Germany
Club: Arsenal (England)
Born: 15 October 1988

86 GAMES — **22 GOALS**

Top skills: Russia 2018 will be Özil's third Finals, after he played every game in both 2014 and 2010. The creative midfielder was as influential as ever in reaching another FIFA World Cup, opening the scoring in a 6-0 win against Norway in September 2017 and playing six qualifiers. Germany's Number 10 makes the game look easy with his pinpoint passing and effective link-up play with the strikers. If goalscorers Thomas Müller, Timo Werner and Mario Gómez are to shoot Germany to a fifth title, they will need all of Özil's skills in orchestrating the midfield.

Ángel di María

Country: Argentina
Club: Paris Saint-Germain (France)
Born: 14 February 1988

90 GAMES — **19 GOALS**

Top skills: An electric winger with fearsome skills, Di María is the man to create chances for strikers Lionel Messi, Sergio Agüero and Gonzalo Higuaín. The left-footed ace can play on either wing but often drifts in from the right to dazzle defenders. At Brazil 2014 Di María had 21 shots on target and made 49 crosses, more than any other player. Had he been fit to play in the Final, Argentina would have had a much better chance of beating Germany. Di María is the finished article on the international stage, but he has unfinished business at the FIFA World Cup Finals.

Nemanja Matić

Country: Serbia
Club: Manchester United (England)
Born: 1 August 1988

36 GAMES — **2 GOALS**

Top skills: Matić has developed from a midfield workhorse into a polished and powerful central midfielder. After returning to Chelsea in 2014 after a successful spell in Portugal, he won two Premier League titles before being snapped up by Manchester United last summer. Much more than just a ball winner and defensive screen, Matić uses his physical presence to join in attacks and has a ferocious long shot. The 2018 FIFA World Cup Finals will be his first, and he goes into the tournament having lost just one of the seven qualifiers he played for Serbia.

Dele Alli

Country: England
Club: Tottenham (England)
Born: 11 April 1996

22 GAMES

2 GOALS

Top skills: If England play with one central striker this summer, then Dele Alli will have a very important role for the Three Lions. The skilful attacking midfielder will play just behind the striker and make runs into the box to test the goalkeeper. Despite only scoring once in qualifiers for Russia 2018, Alli's game is built around scoring and creating chances for his team-mates – before he was 21 he had racked up a mighty 40 goals and assists combined for Tottenham in the Premier League. Alli will be one of the first names on coach Gareth Southgate's team sheet.

16

Alli was just 16 when he played his first professional game for MK Dons, before joining Tottenham in 2015.

FIFA World Cup™ Stars
Defenders

Jan Vertonghen

Country: Belgium
Club: Tottenham (England)
Born: 24 April 1987

97 GAMES | 8 GOALS

Top skills: Playing alongside his Tottenham team-mate Toby Alderweireld, Jan Vertonghen is part of arguably the meanest defence at Russia 2018. With Vertonghen in the team, Belgium conceded just six goals in their ten qualifiers and kept six clean sheets. The tough-tackling centre-back has the experience to keep a cool head in big games and knows when to pick a clever pass from the back to set up attacks. Vertonghen suffered the heartache of quarter-final defeat to Argentina at the 2014 Finals and this time he is targeting a spot beyond that.

Diego Godín

Country: Uruguay
Club: Atlético Madrid (Spain)
Born: 16 February 1986

113 GAMES | 8 GOALS

Top skills: The sight of captain Diego Godín rising high to win a header and score is legendary in Uruguay. The battling centre-back did just that when he put his country into the last 16 at the 2014 Finals, and he bagged three more goals as Uruguay finished second in qualifying to reach Russia. Godín's presence at both ends of the pitch is a key part of coach Óscar Tabárez's game plan. He can stop attacks with a fierce tackle and has tidy footwork to help launch a counter attack. Uruguay's popular Number 3 will be a big influence this summer.

Dani Alves

Country: Brazil
Club: Paris Saint-Germain (France)
Born: 6 May 1983

105 GAMES | 7 GOALS

Top skills: After being part of the squad that crashed out of the 2014 Finals with a 7-1 defeat to Germany, Dani Alves is on a mission in Russia. The experienced right-back has won many titles at club level, including the UEFA Champions League and La Liga with Barcelona and Serie A with Juventus, but he knows that this summer will be his last chance to lift the FIFA World Cup Trophy. Alves will be 35 by the time the tournament kicks off, but no opponent will enjoy taking him on because his stamina, speed and set-piece skills are legendary.

Sergio Ramos

Country: Spain
Club: Real Madrid (Spain)
Born: 30 March 1986

147 GAMES

11 GOALS

Top skills: With a FIFA World Cup, two UEFA European Championships and multiple UEFA Champions League and La Liga crowns, it is easy to see why Sergio Ramos is one of the world's top defenders. Spain's captain and leader remains hungry for more success in Russia and, in the true rampaging Ramos style, he will give opposing strikers a real headache. Even though he turned 32 in 2018, Ramos still has plenty of speed and power to outsmart his opponents. He is a fantastic header of the ball and will fancy his chances of scoring this summer.

100

Ramos made his 100th appearance for Spain aged just 26. He also scored in the game.

FIFA World Cup™ Stars
Goalkeepers

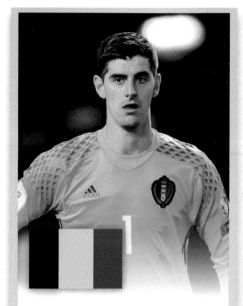

David de Gea

Country: Spain
Club: Manchester United (England)
Born: 7 November 1990

24 GAMES · 2014 DEBUT

Top skills: After failing to make an appearance at the 2014 FIFA World Cup in Brazil, this year De Gea finally gets his big chance to impress on the international stage. The Madrid-born goalkeeper has all the skills needed to shine for Spain in Russia. He is very acrobatic and frequently pulls off miraculous saves, as well as having the confidence to know when to come off his line and shut down an opposition attack. De Gea let in just three goals in qualifying for the Finals and fully deserves to be wearing Spain's Number 1 shirt this summer.

Hugo Lloris

Country: France
Club: Tottenham (England)
Born: 26 December 1986

94 GAMES · 2008 DEBUT

Top skills: No other keeper has as many international caps for France as Hugo Lloris, and for good reason. The shot stopper has a superb all-round game, boasting a strong physical presence and laser-like reflexes. He made a costly mistake in a qualifying defeat to Sweden in June 2017, but showed composure to recover and steer *Les Bleus* to their sixth Finals in a row. Lloris commands his penalty area and gives defenders an ear bashing if needed. He wears the captain's armband with pride and in Russia he will lead France for the fourth time at a major tournament.

Thibaut Courtois

Country: Belgium
Club: Chelsea (England)
Born: 11 May 1992

54 GAMES · 2011 DEBUT

Top skills: Fans may be watching Belgium's attacking talent such as Eden Hazard and Romelu Lukaku this summer, but they should keep an eye on the goalkeeper too. Thibaut Courtois goes into the tournament with a big reputation, having starred for Chelsea and impressed in Belgium's qualifiers – he kept six clean sheets in ten games as his country breezed to the Finals. Of course Courtois has excellent players in front of him but his powers on the goal line, which include stunning saves and calm catching, mark him as a potential superstar at Russia 2018.

Manuel Neuer

Country: Germany
Club: Bayern Munich (Germany)
Born: 27 March 1986

74 GAMES

2009 DEBUT

Top skills: Neuer has been one of the world's best goalkeepers ever since playing at his first FIFA World Cup Finals in 2010. The Bayern Munich captain has everything a modern-day goalkeeper needs, plus plenty more. Neuer is famed for having the intelligence, and bravery, to race from his line and clear attacking threats. This 'sweeper keeper' tactic was very important when Germany lifted the FIFA World Cup Trophy in 2014. Add to this his agility to reach shots, sharp reflexes, accurate kicking and precise long throws, and Neuer really is a force between the posts. At Russia 2018, the defending champions will be very thankful that this man is in action behind their defence!

2016

This was the year Neuer was named Germany captain after Bastian Schweinsteiger retired.

FIFA World Cup™ Quiz: Part 1

Over the next four pages you can really test your FIFA World Cup knowledge with this super-fun quiz. There are 200 points up for grabs in total and you can write your answer by each question. Good luck!

© FIFA TM

10 points for each correct answer

Close Call

The camera has zoomed in on these four teams playing at Russia 2018, but can you name each nation pictured?

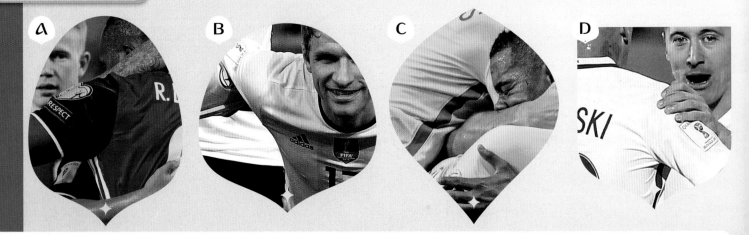

A   **B**   **C**   **D**

Answers:

A...............................   B...............................   C...............................   D...............................

10 points for each correct answer

Top Tens

These FIFA World Cup legends wore number ten at the Finals. Some letters are missing, so write the full name under each.

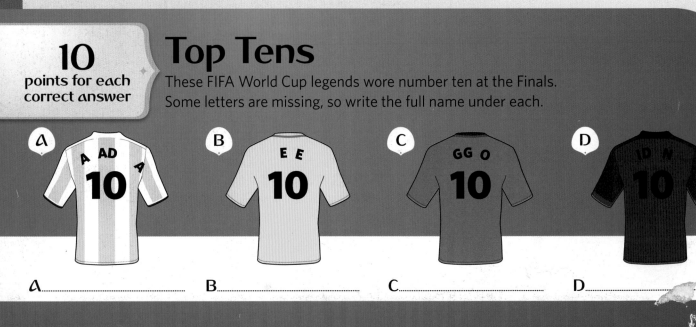

A   A AD   A   **10**   B   E E   **10**   C   GG O   **10**   D   ID N   **10**

A...............................   B...............................   C...............................   D...............................

Golden Goalscorers

James Rodríguez, Thomas Müller and Ronaldo have all won the adidas Golden Boot as top scorer at a FIFA World Cup Finals, but in which year?

10 points for each correct answer

JAMES RODRÍGUEZ	Year ＿ ＿ ＿ ＿
THOMAS MÜLLER	Year ＿ ＿ ＿ ＿
RONALDO	Year ＿ ＿ ＿ ＿

First or Second?

Argentina have won the FIFA World Cup twice, first in 1978 and again in 1986. Are they celebrating their first or second Final victory here?

10 points for the correct answer

1978 ✓   1986 ✓

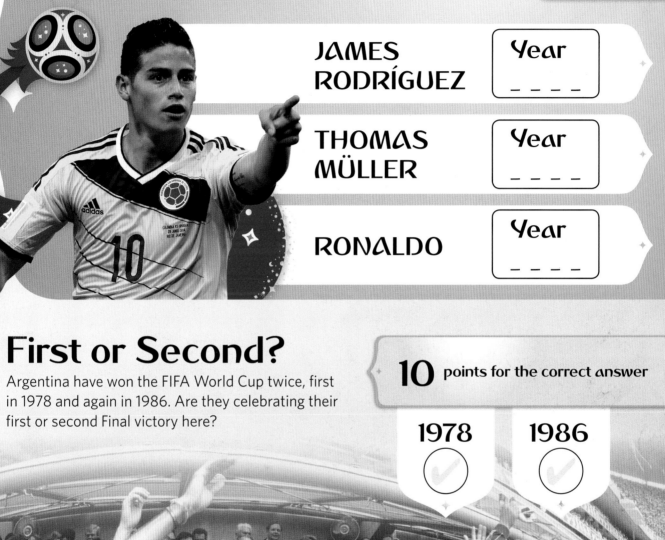

59

FIFA World Cup™ Quiz: Part 2

2
points for each player found

Search for the Stars

Look closely and you will find ten goal stars who have all scored in a FIFA World Cup Final.

```
R E D M Z G S G I B I Q U
S E S C D M E Ö F Q T V I
Y E M O D I R T M X M Y D
M U H P L M R Z I D A N E
Z Ü U M E R O E R B Ö T L
M Z R Q S S N A N I Z D W
U R S L N R A S O N R A C
A B T R E Ö L X E I J M E
Q R R X R R D C J E F L M
E S J A S I O R O S S I H
V L V U E M H V R T B I E
T A G S E Y E I E A G P R
Z P O H N I Z R I A J P B
```

GÖTZE
HURST
INIESTA
JAIRZINHO
ZIDANE
KEMPES
NEESKENS
RONALDO
BREHME
ROSSI

4
points for each correct answer

Penalty Pick

20
points for the correct answer

Italy hero Fabio Grosso is scoring the winning penalty in the 2006 FIFA World Cup Final. Is ball A, B, C or D the real ball?

A ✓
B ✓
C ✓
D ✓

Super Seven

Germany beat Brazil by an amazing score of 7-1 in the semi-final of the 2014 FIFA World Cup. Germany had five goalscorers in the game – tick the five players who scored.

MÜLLER	PODOLSKI
ÖZIL	KROOS
KLOSE	KHEDIRA
LAHM	SCHÜRRLE

Use the Clues

England, Mexico, Spain and Belgium have appeared at lots of FIFA World Cup Finals. Write which of the four countries goes with each fact.

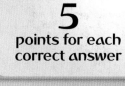
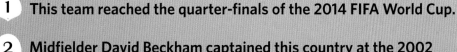

ENGLAND | MEXICO | SPAIN | BELGIUM

1 This team reached the quarter-finals of the 2014 FIFA World Cup.

2 Midfielder David Beckham captained this country at the 2002 and 2006 FIFA World Cup Finals.

3 This country reached their first FIFA World Cup Final in 2010.

4 Russia 2018 will be this nation's 16th appearance at the Finals.

MY FINAL SCORE:

_____ /200

Part 1 Answers

Close Call 1. Belgium; **2.** Germany; **3.** Brazil; **4.** Poland.

Top Tens: Maradona, Pelé, Baggio, Zidane.

Golden Goalscorers: James Rodríguez – 2014; Thomas Müller – 2010; Ronaldo – 2002

First or Second? Second.

Part 2 Answers

Penalty Pick: Ball C

Super Seven: Müller, Klose, Kroos, Khedira, Schürrle.

Use the Clues: 1. Belgium; **2.** England; **3.** Spain; **4.** Mexico.

Search for the Stars

© FIFA TM

Your Match Schedule and Results Chart

Record the results of all 64 group stage and knockout games from the 2018 FIFA World Cup™ Russia. The action begins on 14 June in Moscow with the Final at the Luzhniki Stadium on 15 July.

GROUP A

14 June, 18:00	**Russia** ☐ ☐ **Saudi Arabia**	Moscow
15 June, 17:00	**Egypt** ☐ ☐ **Uruguay**	Ekaterinburg
19 June, 21:00	**Russia** ☐ ☐ **Egypt**	Saint Petersburg
20 June, 18:00	**Uruguay** ☐ ☐ **Saudi Arabia**	Rostov-on-Don
25 June, 18:00	**Uruguay** ☐ ☐ **Russia**	Samara
25 June, 17:00	**Saudi Arabia** ☐ ☐ **Egypt**	Volgograd

Team	P	W	D	L	GD	Pts

GROUP B

15 June, 21:00	**Portugal** ☐ ☐ **Spain**	Sochi
15 June, 18:00	**Morocco** ☐ ☐ **Iran**	Saint Petersburg
20 June, 15:00	**Portugal** ☐ ☐ **Morocco**	Moscow
20 June, 21:00	**Iran** ☐ ☐ **Spain**	Kazan
25 June, 21:00	**Iran** ☐ ☐ **Portugal**	Saransk
25 June, 20:00	**Spain** ☐ ☐ **Morocco**	Kaliningrad

Team	P	W	D	L	GD	Pts

GROUP C

16 June, 13:00	**France** ☐ ☐ **Australia**	Kazan
16 June, 19:00	**Peru** ☐ ☐ **Denmark**	Saransk
21 June, 20:00	**France** ☐ ☐ **Peru**	Ekaterinburg
21 June, 16:00	**Denmark** ☐ ☐ **Australia**	Samara
26 June, 17:00	**Denmark** ☐ ☐ **France**	Moscow
26 June, 17:00	**Australia** ☐ ☐ **Peru**	Sochi

Team	P	W	D	L	GD	Pts

GROUP D

16 June, 16:00	**Argentina** ☐ ☐ **Iceland**	Moscow
16 June, 21:00	**Croatia** ☐ ☐ **Nigeria**	Kaliningrad
21 June, 21:00	**Argentina** ☐ ☐ **Croatia**	Nizhny Novgorod
22 June, 18:00	**Nigeria** ☐ ☐ **Iceland**	Volgograd
26 June, 21:00	**Nigeria** ☐ ☐ **Argentina**	Saint Petersburg
26 June, 21:00	**Iceland** ☐ ☐ **Croatia**	Rostov-on-Don

Team	P	W	D	L	GD	Pts

GROUP E

17 June, 21:00	**Brazil** ☐ ☐ **Switzerland**	Rostov-on-Don
17 June, 16:00	**Costa Rica** ☐ ☐ **Serbia**	Samara
22 June, 15:00	**Brazil** ☐ ☐ **Costa Rica**	Saint Petersburg
22 June, 20:00	**Serbia** ☐ ☐ **Switzerland**	Kaliningrad
27 June, 21:00	**Serbia** ☐ ☐ **Brazil**	Moscow
27 June, 21:00	**Switzerland** ☐ ☐ **Costa Rica**	Nizhny Novgorod

Team	P	W	D	L	GD	Pts

GROUP F

17 June, 18:00	**Germany** ☐ ☐ **Mexico**	Moscow
18 June, 15:00	**Sweden** ☐ ☐ **Korea Republic**	Nizhny Novgorod
23 June, 21:00	**Germany** ☐ ☐ **Sweden**	Sochi
23 June, 18:00	**Korea Republic** ☐ ☐ **Mexico**	Rostov-on-Don
27 June, 17:00	**Korea Republic** ☐ ☐ **Germany**	Kazan
27 June, 19:00	**Mexico** ☐ ☐ **Sweden**	Ekaterinburg

Team	P	W	D	L	GD	Pts